THE WRITINGS ON THE WALL

Peace at the Berlin Wall

Terry Tillman

Foreword by Marilyn Ferguson

22/7
Publishing Company
Santa Monica

Cover photo by Jan Cordes (Ullstein Bilderdienst)
Page 1: Graffito at Pottsdamer Platz. August 1988

First Edition

22/7 PUBLISHING COMPANY
2210 Wilshire Boulevard, Suite 237
Santa Monica, California 90403
(213) 471-2778

ISBN 0-9626551-0-4
Library of Congress Catalog Card Number: 90-90252

Distributed in the United States by
Publishers Group West
4065 Hollis
Emeryville, California 94608
(415) 658-3453

Design: Paul LeBus
Printed in Singapore

For
Timothea,
Kimberly, and Wendy,
with loving and peace.

Contents

Foreward   9

Preface   11

Chapter One   17   The Writings on the Wall

Chapter Two   45   Up Against the Wall

Chapter Three   69   Off the Wall

Chapter Four   93   The Wall Came Tumbling Down

Chapter Five   117   After the Fall

Epilogue   145

Acknowledgements   148

Foreword

Art, it has been said, is where you find it. The painter's eye and the poet's ear select for meaning. This book is richly layered in meaning. We see through the eyes and ears of its creator, through hundreds of graffiti artists, and the poets whose words they often cited. We see photographs of paintings of words, and words that paint pictures.

This book is deeply moving because it is about freedom, an issue central to our longing for a fulfilled life. And it is a model of that freedom. For one thing, it calls our attention to art created from the purest motive: the desire for expression. These artists knew that their creations were likely to be painted over within a few days or hours, so they were not out looking for immortality, or even a product that could be kept, admired, sold, envied.

These were prayers, wails, hosannas, not monuments to human achievement but powerful moments from the human soul. And yet, paradoxically, they can be re-experienced as needed because they were captured in this book. *The Writings on the Wall* has done the impossible, giving the reader the uncanny feeling of actually being in Berlin as the historic event unrolled.

Terry Tillman, the magician who created this experience, is a man of many parts. Reared in a family oriented to business, he started a company at fifteen to sell track hurdles of his own design—the rocker kind now in universal use. He sang with the original New Christy Minstrels, and became involved in business ventures (real estate construction and sales, network and cable television, video production). In the late 1970's, like many other high-achievers, he "did an about-face." After 1977 he traveled the world as a leader of personal growth seminars (first Lifespring, then Insight). He became a full-time student, teacher, and coach in the area of human growth.

It seems characteristic of Terry's thorough-going ways that he has expressed his freedom by generating the ways and means to publish this book in a timely fashion. He felt an urgency about the book's message: That which has been built can be unbuilt, and even the process of dismantling our unworkable structures can be creative, "even the turbulence can be positive." Such grace can help us as we encounter the hurdles along the way.

— *Marilyn Ferguson*

Preface

In August 1961, I had temporarily dropped out of college to begin an adventure as a professional folksinger. John Kennedy was president of the United States. Nikita Kruschev was premier of the Soviet Union. Jet passenger planes were still a marvel. "Skyjacking" was a threat. The Soviets had just orbited Cosmonaut Titov. "To Kill a Mockingbird" was at the top of the moviegoer's list. Short haircuts and "beehive hairdos" were in style; so were pegged pants. Campus protests were in the news. Southern states still had segregated "colored" drinking fountains and toilets.

And the Berlin Wall was erected.

I remember hearing then about the building of the Wall. I probably made a few righteous, judgmental remarks and statements of disbelief. But the Wall was "over there" and didn't seem to affect my day-to-day life. I was separated from that problem by an ocean, a language, my life station, imaginary country boundaries, and history. I had many walls between me and the Berlin Wall. So I really didn't relate to or dwell on the issue. I wasn't very interested in politics, and I thought of the Wall as a political issue.

The Wall was in the news periodically over the subsequent twenty-eight years. Occasionally the information was about brutal, compassionless incidents at the Wall. I just filed those away inside someplace where I record Man's inhumanity to Man, and went on about my business.

It wasn't until the summer of 1988 that I visited Berlin and the Wall. I was initially surprised at the profundity of my experience. As I drove through the city I imagined it whole and full of the richness of life as it might have been in the 19th century. The image seemed real. Then I had a flood of emotion. It was like the city was a broken heart, two halves split, and I was feeling the hurt of that inside me. Something in me connected at a deep level with Berlin, this symbol of human separation.

When I got to the Wall, I was incredulous. "Incomprehensible! Do people know about this thing? Can they really know without witnessing it firsthand?" I said to nobody in particular. "Do they really believe they can keep people separated by a physical wall?" In my brain the Wall just did not compute.

I climbed onto an observation platform so that I could see over the Wall. On the other side was a "no man's land," a swath cleared through the middle of the city. On the other side of this zone was a second wall. Between the walls, in no man's land, at intervals of perhaps 400 meters, were guard towers. There were East German soldiers glaring from the towers. They looked threatening and ominous. I later learned that one thousand two hundred trained "wolf hounds" also guarded no man's land. It was mined as well. In some places the Wall went right up against buildings, and the buildings were used as part of the Wall. Sometimes an existing building was one half in East Berlin and one half in West Berlin. Incomprehensible.

My companions and I took some time to meditate and to imagine the Wall disappearing, disintegrating, and being replaced with bike paths and parks full of people together in joy. A part of me wondered if our efforts could really accomplish anything. Another part said, "What the heck, so far the other approaches to ending the division hadn't accomplished anything."

I walked about three miles along the Wall during this visit. What I first noticed were the graffiti. They communicated a message that was colorful, poetic, humorous, artistic, prophetic, loving, hopeful, frustrated, and rarely hateful. I felt inspired and enthusiastic. "Neat," I thought. "Someone ought to take pictures of this and put it in a book," I said. "I'll bet most of the world has no idea this is here. You could call the book *Off The Wall*, or *The Writings on the Wall* or *Up Against the Wall*." I even thought about hiring a student to walk the Wall each week to take pictures of any new graffiti.

I have a great many ideas, and most, naturally, don't materialize. I jotted this idea in a section in my calendar planning book where I record ideas. I had a deep rich experience in Berlin that summer.

I left and went about my business.

Almost two years passed with only an occasional thought about my "idea" for a book on the Wall. Then, on November 9, 1989, I was leading a seminar in Los Angeles. As I was sitting in front of the room on a stool, an associate brought me a note: "The Berlin Wall just came down." She had known that somehow the Wall was important to me. I made no attempt to hide the tears of joy rolling down my face as I announced the news to the group. The emotional connection I had experienced during my first visit to Berlin and the Wall returned.

I have at least a partial idea of why I'm deeply connected to the events in Berlin and around the Wall. For thirteen years I have devoted my life to presenting seminars that teach people how to remove their personal walls. Participants learn how to produce more of whatever they want. Often they discover that what they really want is measured subjectively rather than objectively. At a deeper level they are looking for peace of mind, joy, an experience of security, confidence, higher self-esteem, freedom, better relationships, loving.

Those of us who do this work are often romantic idealists. We dream of a peaceful and loving world as a real possibility—not just a few weeks around Christmas time, but most of the time. And yet we're practical. There is much work to be done, so we do what we can, small bit by bit. Sometimes I wonder if I'm really contributing, whether my efforts make a difference. And then an event like the opening of the Berlin Wall occurs and I'm reminded of why I do what I do. If enough of us do our little bit after all, then added together we do make a difference. The whole is the sum of the parts.

Something in my heart commanded me to

Berlin. My brain said, "You're too busy. You finally have a chance to relax at home for a change. Why get in another airplane. It costs too much money. It's really none of your business." Chatter, chatter, chatter. So, of course, I decided to fly to Berlin. Once I committed to go, the magic began (and it's continued on this project right up to this day).

As you can imagine, the world was descending on Berlin. The first three airlines I called were full as were most of the hotels in Berlin. The fourth airline had seats available only in First Class. I didn't want to pay First Class fares. Somehow the ticketing agent agreed to give me the First Class tickets for the Coach price, all the while repeating, "We don't do this." as she wrote the ticket. The same thing happened in the hotel. I was installed in a suite for the fare of a smaller room, because the suite was the only room available.

I'm not a professional photographer and I wanted to get excellent quality pictures. I asked my friend David Mackenzie, a world class professional photographer, if he wanted to join me. He seemed excited and interested and began making his arrangements.

The editor for a small Los Angeles-based newspaper, *The New Day Herald,* heard I was going to Berlin. She offered to have some of their business cards printed identifying me as a reporter (I had written several articles for that paper). She said the cards might get me admission to sites that were otherwise off limits. The director of the Institute for Individual and World Peace also called to offer some of their cards with my name on them.

I needed a translator. I have friends in Germany but none of them were available for more than an hour or two a day. Then I thought of my younger sister, Nancy Romalov, who has taught German in college and who has lived in Berlin. But there was a problem. Nancy and I had one eight year period without speaking to each other. One of the last communications I had received from her was second hand, and that was that she was thinking of suing me over some family business and was apparently quite upset with me. I didn't know why. I had always liked Nancy and yet I had not made much effort to communicate or share with her.

I called Nancy. At first she seemed to think the idea was interesting but out of the question. She gave me all the reasons why she couldn't go—reasons that sounded like *my* brain chatter. Yet she overcame her considerations and agreed to meet me in Berlin.

At the last minute David cancelled his plans to go. At that point I very nearly gave up the project. I was flooded with doubts. I couldn't take pictures good enough for a book, I told myself. I was not a photographer, maybe I shouldn't go. Yet I grabbed my camera and thirty-five rolls of film. After all, if necessary I could buy pictures from newspapers or other photographers.

Within two days after the original decision to go I was in Berlin. I was caught up at once in the excitement and celebration that pervaded the city. The sense of freedom was palpable. Here was a preview of the peaceful, joyful city of my dreams—a preview of the possibility of peace.

I went immediately to the Brandenburg Gate, the symbolic image of the Wall presented through the news media, and now the center of activity. The crowds were immense. A press bleacher had been erected at the gate—platforms eight to twenty-five feet above the ground. These were primarily for international television. The press platforms offered the only viewing spot above the crowds where pictures were possible. Guards and barriers blocked the platform. I flashed my *New Day Herald* business card identifying me as a reporter and they let me in! NBC, CBS, ABC, CNN, BBC, Japanese TV crews and others, and Terry Tillman of *The New Day Herald.*

The next day I went to the Checkpoint Charlie Museum. This is the archive for the Wall—history, artifacts, and information. I arrived as a press conference was in progress and got in with my magic card. I met many people who had escaped over or under the Wall. I met an East German soldier who had become international news when he was photographed jumping over the barbed wire in 1961. I met artists who had painted on the Wall. Here were the human stories of the Wall.

My sister and I laughed, talked and cleared some of our own history. We had some touching moments together. She translated skillfully, guided me and supported me. As the Berlin Wall began coming down the barriers between us crumbled. While we grew up in the kind of family where we seldom, if ever, said directly "I love you," that message was communicated in other ways during our time together.

Ironically, although the Berlin Wall is a symbol of divisiveness, it was—and is—a place where people congregate for meaningful communication. It is analogous to what biologists call an "ecotone." An ecotone is the area of transition between "ecological communities." The biologists say that many of the most interesting things happen at the ecotone. A beach—the meeting of land and sea—is an ecotone. A beach is a zone of play, integration, change, interaction, conflict, turbulence, and transformation. The Wall, too, is an ecotone. It is an area and instrument of both separation and unity.

This book is about more than the Berlin Wall, its graffiti, and how it came to be opened. It is about the walls in our daily lives, how these add up to a fragmented world, and how, bit by bit (peace by peace?), we can free our world. It is witness to a consciousness change from division and separation to unity, oneness, and human caring. It's about the family of man. And it is a record of the demonstration of the very real possibility of individual and world peace. The writing's on the wall.

Chapter One

The Writings on the Wall

Before it began to be dismantled, the Berlin Wall was approximately one hundred and five miles long encircling the city. About forty five miles of the Wall was built of concrete. During several visits I walked or rode a bicycle along thirty of those miles and I was never out of site of graffiti. The graffiti were only on the West Berlin side of the Wall. In many places the graffiti is many layers deep. And most of it is only visible for a short time (often just a few days) because it is painted over by the next artist. The writing on the Wall seems to appear mysteriously. During the more than two hundred hours I spent near the Wall over fifteen days, I did not once see anyone painting on the Wall.

The message and experience of the writing on the Berlin Wall is strangely uplifting. It is a touching chronicle of human creativity, determination, hope, and unity. It seemed inevitable that the Wall would eventually come down. The graffiti prophesied that—literally the writing was on the wall. And the opening of the Wall is more than just the removal of a physical barrier and division. It is a joining, coming together of human consciousness. A new unity that is only possible when we love our diversity.

How many years can a mountain exist
before it's washed to the sea?
How many years can some people exist
before they're allowed to be free?
How many times can a man turn his head
pretending he just doesn't see?

The answer my friend is blowing in the wind
The answer is blowing in the wind.

BOB DYLAN
"BLOWIN' IN THE WIND" (1963)

All great questions must be raised by great voices, and the greatest voice is the voice of the people—speaking out in prose, or painting, or poetry, or music; speaking out in homes and halls, streets and farms, courts and cafes—let that voice speak and the stillness you hear will be the gratitude of mankind.

ROBERT KENNEDY (1963)

All free men, wherever they may live, are citizens of Berlin. And therefore, as a free man, I take pride in the words *Ich bin ein Berliner.*

JOHN FITZGERALD KENNEDY
AT WEST BERLIN CITY HALL (1963)

Liberty is a thing of the spirit.

Herbert Hoover

If everyone sweeps before his own front door, then the street is clean.

JOHANN WOLFGANG VON GOETHE

Man must evolve for all human conflict a method which rejects revenge, aggression and retaliation. The foundation of such a method is love.

MARTIN LUTHER KING, JR.

"Love thy neighbor as thyself,"
It would be splendid to think
Christ's message about loving
our neighbors as ourselves
might at last be heeded.

Queen Elizabeth II
on East Bloc change
(December 25, 1989)

Anyone who chooses to live their life
in Loving can change the world.

JOHN-ROGER

Lord, make us instruments of Thy peace. Where there is hatred, let us sow love; where there is injury, pardon; where there is discord, union; where there is doubt, faith; where there is despair, hope; where there is darkness, light; where there is sadness, joy.

ST. FRANCIS OF ASSISI

Even in areas behind the curtain, that which Jefferson called
"the disease of liberty" still appears to be infectious.

JOHN FITZGERALD KENNEDY (1962)

We look forward to the time when the power of Love will replace the love of Power. Then will our world know the blessings of Peace.

WILLIAM EWART GLADSTONE

Sometime they'll give a war and
nobody will come.

CARL SANDBURG
THE PEOPLE, YES

There is a strong shadow
where there is much light.

JOHANN WOLFGANG VON GOETHE

There are two ways
of spreading light:
to be the candle
or the mirror that reflects it.

EDITH WHARTON

Chapter Two

Up Against the Wall

It seems that the East German authorities were "up against the wall" with their strategies of physical division and restriction of freedom. The Wall was a dead end approach. Yet there were "four generations" of Wall since the first was built in 1961—each built higher, thicker and stronger.

From the founding of the DDR (East Germany) until the Wall opened, over three million—one-sixth of its population—have fled over its border to the West. Sixty thousand were arrested for planning or attempting to flee. There were fifty thousand East German Soldiers on the border through Germany. Two thousand of those escaped between 1961 and 1966. Over one hundred and twenty citizens were killed attempting to escape to the West over, under, through, or around the Wall. The most recent casualty was in May 1989.

The East German government spent an average of over $6,000,000 each year to maintain the Wall. When I heard that statistic I wondered how much energy I spend each year supporting my walls of opinions, superiority, inferiority, hurt, judgment, resentment, anger, fear....

A permanent peace cannot be prepared by threats but only by the honest attempt to create mutual trust. However strong national armaments may be, they do not create military security for any nation nor do they guarantee the maintenance of peace.

ALBERT EINSTEIN

Ah! when shall all men's good
Be each man's rule,
    and universal Peace
Lie like a shaft of light
    across the land?

ALFRED, LORD TENNYSON

49

To all new truths, or renovation of old truths, it must be as in the ark between the destroyed and the about-to-be renovated world. The raven must be sent out before the dove, and ominous controversy must precede peace and the olive wreath.

SAMUEL TAYLOR COLERIDGE

I think that people want peace so much that one of these days government had better get out of the way and let them have it.

DWIGHT D. EISENHOWER

Psalm 21, Verse 11, ran:
"For they intended evil against thee;
they imagined a mischievous device,
which they are not able to perform."

JOHN FITZGERALD KENNEDY

When armies are mobilized and issues are joined,
The man who is sorry over the fact will win.

LAO-TZU

We are not enemies, but friends. Though passion may have strained, it must not break our bonds of affection. The mystic chords of memory, stretching from every battlefield and patriot grave to every living heart and hearthstone all over this broad land, will yet swell the chorus of the Union when again touched, as surely they will be, by the better angels of our nature.

ABRAHAM LINCOLN

We are not here to curse the darkness, but to light the candle that can guide us through that darkness to a safe and sane future.

"Peace upon earth!" was said. We sing it,
And pay a million priests to bring it.
After two thousand years of mass
We've got as far as poison-gas.

THOMAS HARDY
(CHRISTMAS 1924)

I am the enemy you killed, my friend.

WILFRED OWEN

I have cherished the ideal of a democratic and free society in which all persons live together in harmony and with equal opportunities. It is an ideal which I hope to live for and to achieve. But, if needs be, it is an ideal for which I am prepared to die.

NELSON MANDELA

Do you know what amazes me more than anything else?—the impotence of force to organize anything. There are only two powers in the world—the spirit and the sword; and in the long run the sword will always be conquered by the spirit.

NAPOLEON BONAPARTE

The spirit of man is more important than mere physical strength, and the spiritual fiber of a nation than its wealth.

DWIGHT D. EISENHOWER

Chapter Three

Off the Wall

Really, the writer doesn't want success.
He knows he has a short span of life,
that the day will come
when he must pass through the wall of oblivion,
and he wants to leave a scratch on that wall
—Kilroy was here—
that somebody a hundred, or a thousand years later will see.

William Faulkner

"Off the Wall" is American slang meaning bizarre, absurd, loony, preposterous, silly, zany, outlandish, funny, unconventional, offbeat, different. Much of the graffiti in on the Berlin Wall were certainly all of that and more. Most were entertaining and provocative. Here's a sampling.

"And hast thou slain the Jabberwock?
Come to my arms, my beamish boy!
O frabjous day Calloh! Callay!"
He chortled in his joy.

Lewis Carroll
Through the Looking Glass

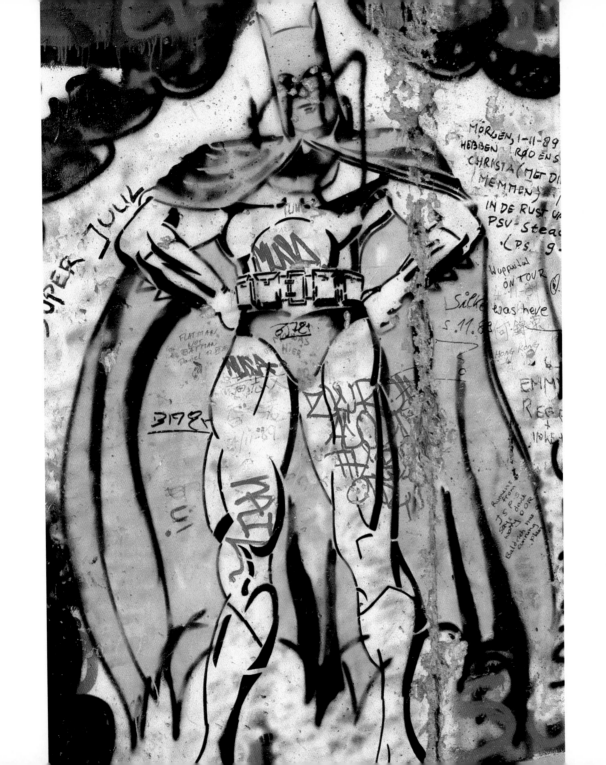

The only devils in this world are those running around in our own hearts, and that is where all our battles should be fought.

MOHANDAS (MAHATMA) GANDHI

Imagine there's no heaven
It's easy if you try
No hell below us
Above us only sky
Imagine all the people
living for today
Imagine there's no countries
It isn't hard to do
Nothing to kill or die for
and no religion too
Imagine all the people
living life in peace

You may say I'm a dreamer
But I'm not the only one
I hope someday you'll join us
And the world will live as one
Imagine no possessions
I wonder if you can
No need for greed or hunger
A brotherhood of man
Imagine all the people
Sharing all the world
You may say I'm a dreamer
But I'm not the only one
I hope someday you'll join us
And the world will live as one

JOHN LENNON
"IMAGINE" (1971)

Humpty Dumpty sat on a wall.
Humpty Dumpty had a great fall.
All the king's horses and all the king's men
Couldn't put Humpty together again.

Liberty has never come from government. Liberty has always come from the subjects of it.

WOODROW WILSON

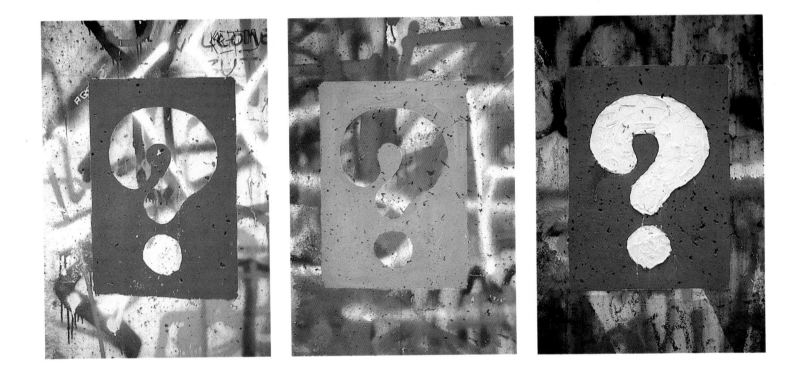

What is the answer? (I was silent.)
In that case, what is the question?

GERTRUDE STEIN
LAST WORDS
FROM ALICE B. TOKLAS *WHAT IS REMEMBERED*

It is better to know some of the questions
than all of the answers.

JAMES THURBER

BEAT
CAL

TINY PURPLE FISHES RUN
LAUGHING THRU YOUR FINGERS

Fuck off and HIDE

TRS
7312

ENDLICH
10.11.1989

DIE MAUER
DIE MAUER

DIVISION

DECADES

GEBURT
AB NF

We will march forward to a better tomorrow so long as separate groups like the blacks, the negros, and the coloreds can come together to work out their differences.

STEVE ALLEN

There is nothing either good or bad,
but thinking makes it so.

WILLIAM SHAKESPEARE

Before I built a wall I'd ask to know
What I was walling in or walling out.

ROBERT FROST
"MENDING WALL"

I'm starting with the man in the mirror.
I'm asking him to change his ways.
And no message could have been any clearer:
If you want to make the world a better place
Take a look at yourself, then make the change.

SIEDAH GARRETT AND GLEN BALLARD
"MAN IN THE MIRROR"

*Mirrors should reflect a little
before throwing back images.*

Jean Cocteau

Chapter Four

The Wall Came Tumbling Down

New border crossings at the Wall opened on November 9, 1989. The actual physical disassembling of the Wall began in February 1990. I returned to Berlin on the precise day in February when the dismantling began.

Most of the activity at the Wall has been along an approximate two-mile section between the Brandenburg Gate and Checkpoint Charlie (a crossing into East Berlin located in the American sector). As you approach the Wall, before it is visible, you hear the sound of metal chipping against concrete, a chorus of thousands of people hacking at the Wall to get a souvenir and perhaps to hasten the removal. Prior to November 9, 1989, that would have been a life-threatening activity.

I met people of all ages, sizes, colors, and nationalities, joyfully walking up and down the Wall, greeting each other and occasionally working to get their own "piece of the rock". When I returned in February, enterprising citizens from many countries had set up small stands to sell pieces of the Wall. The pieces were selling for $2 to $20 depending on size and packaging. And hundreds were buying.

The actual removal process will take some time. It has taken two months to remove a two-mile section. The present Wall is made up of four foot wide concrete sections, thirteen-and-a-half feet tall and six inches thick. Each section weighs approximately four tons. The concrete is laced inside with one-inch steel reinforcement bar every four inches. It was obviously built to be indestructible.

How long will it take to remove the intangible, invisibly subjective walls inside the people?

Come mothers and fathers throughout the land

And don't criticize what you can't understand.

Your sons and your daughters are beyond your command.

Your old world is rapidly aging.

Please get out of the new one if you can't lend a hand.

For the times they are a changin'.

BOB DYLAN
"THE TIMES THEY ARE A CHANGIN'" (1963)

My work will be finished if I succeed in carrying conviction to the human family that every man or woman, however weak in body, is the guardian of his or her self-respect and liberty. This defense avails, though the whole world may be against that individual resister.

MOHANDAS (MAHATMA) GANDHI

If we are to reach real peace in this world and if we are to carry on a real war against war, we shall have to begin with children; and if they will grow up in their natural innocence, we won't have to struggle; we won't have to pass fruitless idle resolutions, but we shall go from love to love and peace to peace, until at last all the corners of the world are covered with that peace and love for which consciously or unconsciously the whole world is hungering.

MOHANDAS (MAHATMA) GANDHI

We will prove to the world that we believe in peacefully "tearing down walls" instead of arbitrarily building them.

JOHN FITZGERALD KENNEDY

GET A PIECE
OF THE ROCK
TAKE DOWN
THIS WALL!

This world demands the qualities of youth;
not a time of life but a state of mind, a temper
of the will, a quality of the imagination, a
predominance of courage over timidity, or the
appetite for adventure over the love of ease.
It is a revolutionary world we live in, and thus,
as I have said in Latin America and Asia,
in Europe and in the United States,
it is young people who must take the lead.

ROBERT KENNEDY (1966)

Lay me on an anvil, O God.

Beat me and hammer me into a crowbar.

Let me pry loose old walls.

Let me lift and loosen old foundations.

CARL SANDBURG
"PRAYERS OF STEEL"

Stone walls do not a prison make,
Nor iron bars a cage;
Minds innocent and quiet take
That for an hermitage;
If I have freedom in my love,
And in my soul am free,
Angels alone that soar above
Enjoy such liberty.

RICHARD LOVELACE

Mark! where his carnage and his conquests cease!
He makes a solitude, and calls it—peace!

LORD BYRON

It never occurred to her that if the drainpipes of a house are clogged, the rain may collect in pools on the roof; and she suspected no danger until suddenly she discovered a crack in the wall.

GUSTAVE FLAUBERT
MADAME BOVARY

What a beautiful fix we are in now; peace has been declared.

NAPOLEON BONAPARTE

Chapter Five

After the Fall

For a sustained moment the world glimpsed a possible future, life after the Wall. Animosities seemed to dissolve, former enemies behaved like friends.

In the first days East German soldiers, who had once operated under orders to shoot those trying to climb over the Wall or burrow under it, tended to be awkward, unsure how to respond to the new reality. In November they were still ordering people away from the Wall with occasional sternness, yet by February they were helping people climb onto the Wall.

And then there were the "trained-killer" wolfhounds. Shortly after the first opening in the Wall the East German government announced that ninety percent of the dogs were not trained to attack at all. More than a thousand of these "fierce" wolfhounds are now family pets.

Some sites along the Wall have become playgrounds and meeting places where strangers join in celebration. Will it last? Will we rise to the challenges and work ahead? I believe we will. The handwriting is on the wall. As Anne Frank said in 1944, "I believe that people are really good at heart. I think it will all come right, that this cruelty too will end, and that peace and tranquility will return again."

"I can't wait for peace. Can you?"
Faunia Fox, age six

The Bible teaches quite unequivocally that people are created for fellowship, for togetherness; not for alienation, apartness, enmity, and division

ARCHBISHOP DESMOND TUTU

Looking through chiseled hole in Wall,
viewing newly opened gate at Potsdamer Platz,
one of the busiest intersections in Berlin
before World War II.

Peaceful circulation has been
interrupted by barbed wire
and concrete blocks. For a city
or a people to be truly free,
they must have the secure right,
without economic, political
or police pressure, to make
their own choice and
to live their own lives.

JOHN FITZGERALD KENNEDY (1961)

We no longer think we are always right. We have now decided, firmly and un-equivocally, to base our policy on the principle of freedom of choice.

MIKHAIL GORBACHEV (1989)

Peeking into "no man's land"

Every exit is an entry
somewhere else.

TOM STOPPARD

The earth is a depot, where wingless angels
pass the time waiting for the long ride home.
Seeing a small boy smiling in the corner I said,
"You must be anxious to go home."
"I am home," he replied, "I just come here to play the games".

Oliver Makin

By my God I leaped over a wall.

2 SAMUEL 22:30

You must give some time to your fellow man. Even if it's a little thing, do something for those who have need of help, something for which you get no pay but the privilege of doing it. For remember, you don't live in a world all your own. Your brothers are here, too.

ALBERT SCHWEITZER

There was so much handwriting on the wall that even the wall fell down.

CHRISTOPHER MORLEY

At a time of tumultuous change we have to remain confident and look to the positive results, and decide which walls should be destroyed and which should be built.

MIKHAIL GORBACHEV (1989)

And it came to pass, when the people heard the sound of the trumpet, and the people shouted with a great shout, that the wall fell down flat, so that the people went up into the city.

JOSHUA 6:20

Like flowing through a broken dam,
East Germans flood into West Berlin.

Citizens of the world walking under Brandenburg Gate, originially a victory monument, for the first time in twenty-eight years

The individual isn't quite an individual, he is a branch of a plant. Jesus uses this image when he says, "I am the vine and you are the branches."

JOSEPH CAMPBELL

As we are part of the land, you too are part of the land. The earth is precious to us. It is also precious to you. One thing we know; there is only one God. No man, be he Red Man or White Man, can be apart. We are brothers after all.

CHIEF SEATTLE
DUWAMISH TRIBE

Peace, peace on earth, goodwill to men, real peace, real goodwill is more of a goal than a reality. Until truly there is goodwill among men, not a wall to divide them, our pursuit of peace shall continue. The Christmas lights of free Berlin cast a glow which penetrates deep into the darkness surrounding. No wall can keep out this light. We know that this beacon will continue to shine brightly for many years to come.

JOHN FITZGERALD KENNEDY
CHRISTMAS MESSAGE TO THE PEOPLE OF WEST BERLIN
(DECEMBER 25, 1961)

From where the sun now stands I will fight no more forever.

CHIEF JOSEPH
NEZ PERCE TRIBE

Now join hands
and with your hands your hearts

William Shakespeare

Epilogue

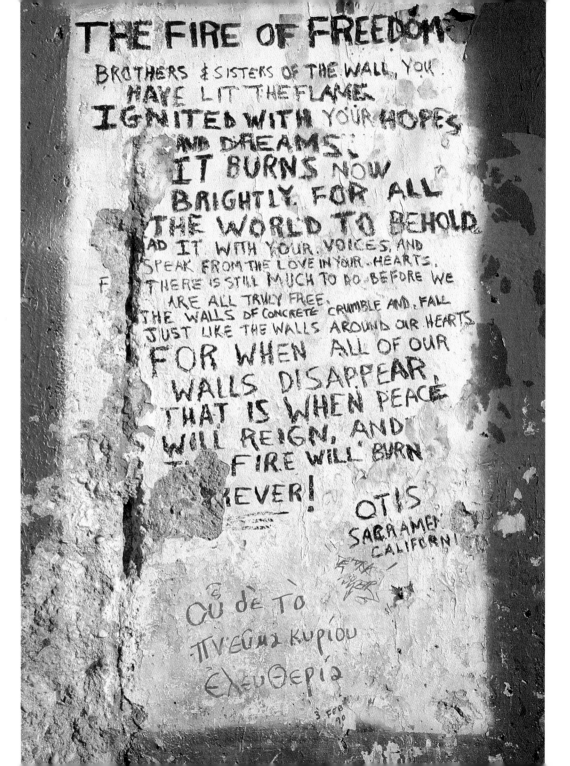

THE FIRE OF FREEDOM

BROTHERS & SISTERS OF THE WALL, YOU
HAVE LIT THE FLAME.
IGNITED WITH YOUR HOPES
AND DREAMS.
IT BURNS NOW
BRIGHTLY FOR ALL
THE WORLD TO BEHOLD.
AD IT WITH YOUR VOICES, AND
SPEAK FROM THE LOVE IN YOUR HEARTS.
THERE IS STILL MUCH TO DO BEFORE WE
ARE ALL TRULY FREE.
THE WALLS OF CONCRETE CRUMBLE AND FALL
JUST LIKE THE WALLS AROUND OUR HEARTS

FOR WHEN ALL OF OUR
WALLS DISAPPEAR,
THAT IS WHEN PEACE
WILL REIGN, AND
FIRE WILL BURN
REVER!

OTIS
SACRAMEN
CALIFORNI

Ou dè tò
πνευμα κυρίου
Έλευθερία

147

Acknowledgements

*Sometimes our light goes out but is blown again into flame
by an encounter with another human being.
Each of us owes the deepest thanks to those
who have rekindled this inner light.*

Albert Schweitzer

The inner light of my enthusiasm for this project was blown into a flame time and again by other people. I am humbled by their willingness to set aside their own commitments to support this project, knowing that it was more than one person could accomplish. Among those who helped greatly: Paul LeBus, who added his artistic talent and shepherded me through the process of design and production. David MacKenzie, who educated me in the editing of photos and kept my idealistic vision alive. Brian O'Leary, whose editorial assistance, friendship and experience eased my way. Peter Scott who modeled unconditional service. Sam Westmacott, who gets results with heart.

The wonderful Germans who made sure I never felt lost and lonely: Klaus Frey; Wolfgang and Lauren Bauermeister; Beneditka Ritgen (hostess, guide, and interpreter); Rainer Hildebrandt, director of the Checkpoint Charlie Museum.

Nancy Romalov, my sister, who had the courage (literally, the heart) to join me in Berlin. Our time together is one of the significant and enduring consequences of this adventure.

Because I had never before produced a book, I had much to learn. Peter McWilliams gave me "quick courses" on publishing and writing, Arianna Stassinopoulos Huffington shared her wisdom and experience, as well as invaluable introductions in the publishing world, and Marilyn Ferguson unselfishly rearranged her busy days to give me expert input on rewriting. Virginia Hopkins and Victoria Marine assisted with last-minute editing and proofreading. Thanks, too, to Lori Comtois and Dave Smith at Palace Press and Charles Winton and Julie Bennett of Publishers Group West.

Valuable feedback, information and direction came from Paul Gottlieb, Glenn Yarbrough, Phil Pochoda, Nancy Andrews, Lila Rolantz, Michael Mindlin, Becky Cabaza, Sam Green, Steve Tennis, Leigh Taylor-Young, Jan Shepherd and Katherine Hall.

Many others assisted me with their ongoing support, encouragement and friendship: Kim Tillman, Wendy Tillman, Cara Barker, Ivan Weinberg, Martha Boston-MacKenzie, Mary Ann Summerville, Lawrence Caminite, Merle Dulien, Sonny Henry, Sally Kirkland, Pat Hyduk, Gail and George Martin-Mauser, Dave Ellingson, Hal Ayotte, and Rob Mills.

John-Roger, (founder of Insight Seminars and the Institute for Individual and World Peace), has been a wayshower to me with his mystical ability to magically engage me in learning through process and experience.

Timothea Stewart, my partner and friend, has inspired me through her demonstration of devotion and integrity, and encouraged me to reach ever higher.

A portion of the proceeds from the sale of this book is being donated to the
INSTITUTE FOR INDIVIDUAL AND WORLD PEACE,
a non-profit organization promoting the idea that
as individuals find inner peace we will experience greater peace in the world.
For information, write them at
2101 Wilshire Boulevard, Santa Monica, California 90403,
or call (213) 828-0535.

Photo Credits

Page	53	Manfred Klockner (Ullstein Bilderdienst)
Page	63	Manfred Klockner (Ullstein Bilderdienst)
Page	91	Harry Delighter
Page	132	Jurgen Engler (Ullstein Bilderdienst)
Page	134	Gunter Peters (Ullstein Bilderdienst)
Page	137	Herbert Schlemmer (Ullstein Bilderdienst)
Page	139	Hans-Albert Scherhaufer (Ullstein Bilderdienst)
Page	141	Jan Cordes (Ullstein Bilderdienst)
Page	143	Hans-Albert Scheraufer (Ullstein Bilderdienst)
Page	152	Betty Bennett

All other photographs by Terry Tillman

TERRY TILLMAN has led personal growth, effectiveness, motivation and leadership seminars for over 30,000 people during the past 13 years. His work has taken him to 40 cities and 26 countries. His simple uncompromising philosophy of the limitless abundance available in life, and his quest to experience purpose, loving and peace has led him into a variety of environments. From the time he started his first business manufacturing track hurdles at the age of 15 to his current work designing workshops on the leading edge of the human potential movement, Terry has had many adventures. He has been on television, records, and on international tours as a singer, banjo player and original member of the New Christy Minstrels folk group. After graduating from Stanford University with a degree in Economics, he founded a real estate development, construction and sales company. He became a member of the Million Dollar Sales Club his first year in 1966. He has been a part owner and Director of a network of television stations, a satellite cable business and a video production company. He holds a private pilot's license, has been a white water rafting guide, a ski instructor, and a marathon runner. Terry now travels eight to ten months each year, primarily for Insight Seminars. He presents and designs seminars, trains seminar leaders and assists people to produce results, discover their value and realize their dreams. His current interest and focus is in promoting individual and world peace, and in removing personal walls (his and others).